MW00354634

D'Nealian® Handwriting
Practice and
Review Workbook

Letter Review

Connections Practice

Grammar and Writing Practice

4

Scott Foresman - Addison Wesley

D'Nealian® Handwriting is a registered trademark of Donald Neal Thurber.

ISBN: 0-673-59284-7

Copyright ©   Addison Wesley Educational Publishers Inc.

All rights reserved. Printed in the United States of America.

This publication is protected by copyright and permission should be obtained from the
publisher prior to any prohibited reproduction, storage in a retrieval system, or transmission
in any form or by any means, electronic, mechanical, photocopying, recording, or otherwise.
For information regarding permission, write to: Scott Foresman - Addison Wesley,
1900 East Lake Avenue, Glenview, Illinois 60025.

Contents

Name _____

The Size of Letters

Look at the size of the letters.

L   l   J   j   I   i

- Capital letters and tall lower-case letters are the same size.

B   b   H   h   K   k

- Short lower-case letters are half the size of tall lower-case letters.

e   o   n   c   a   w

- Many letters stop up at the bottom line.

d   A   r   s   x   M

- Some letters go below the bottom line.

g   j   p   q   y   z

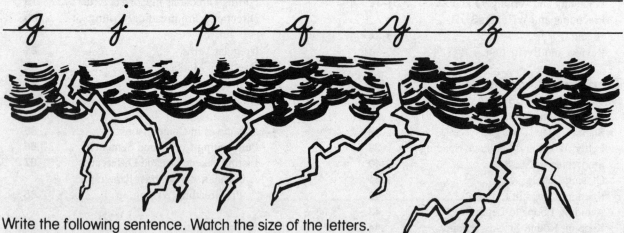

Write the following sentence. Watch the size of the letters.
  Lightning flashed across the black sky.

_____

_____

_____

Now look at the letters in your sentence. Are the letters the
correct size? Circle any letters that are not the correct size.
Practice them on a piece of paper.

4

© Scott Foresman - Addison Wesley

Name

Common Handwriting Problems

Mistakes in handwriting can make what you have written
difficult to read. Look at these common handwriting problems.
Read what to do to about them.

- Close round letters completely.

o not v   lock not lvck

- Keep the loop open in a letter with a loop.

l not l   lake not lake

- Be sure to round the tops of round letters.

m not w   met not wet

- Do not add a loop to a letter that doesn't need one.

i not e   big not beg

Write these words.

clouds _____   thunder _____

rain _____   storm _____

weather _____   sunlight _____

Look at the words you wrote. Did you write each letter correctly?

© Scott Foresman - Addison Wesley

Name _____

Personal Style

Your handwriting is different from the handwriting of everyone else. Look at the handwriting of four different people below. The styles are different but the writing is readable.

• Writing with no slant

Rain danced on the rooftops.

• Writing that slants left

Rain danced on the rooftops.

• Small writing

Rain danced on the rooftops.

• Large writing

Rain danced on the rooftops.

Write the sentence from above.

_____

_____

Ask a friend to look at your writing. Is your writing readable?
What is your personal style?

© Scott Foresman - Addison Wesley

Evaluating Your Handwriting

Copy the following poem. Then evaluate your writing.

Rain

The rain is raining all around,
It falls on field and tree,
It rains on the umbrellas here,
And on the ships at sea.

by Robert Louis Stevenson

_____

_____

_____

_____

_____

Use these questions to evaluate your writing.

	Yes	No
Do all the letters slant in the same direction?	☐	☐
Are the letters shaped correctly?	☐	☐
Are the letters the correct size?	☐	☐
Are the letters spaced evenly?	☐	☐
Is the writing smooth and even?	☐	☐

© Scott Foresman - Addison Wesley

Manuscript Letter Descriptions

Lower-case Letters

a — Middle start; around down, close up, down, and a monkey tail.

b — Top start; slant down, around, up, and a tummy.

c — Start below the middle; curve up, around, down, up, and stop.

d — Middle start; around down, touch, up high, down, and a monkey tail.

e — Start between the middle and bottom; curve up, around, touch, down, up, and stop.

f — Start below the top; curve up, around, and slant down. Cross.

g — Middle start; around down, close up, down under water, and a fishhook.

h — Top start; slant down, up over the hill, and a monkey tail.

i — Middle start; slant down and a monkey tail. Add a dot.

j — Middle start; slant down under water and a fishhook. Add a dot.

k — Top start; slant down, up into a little tummy, and a monkey tail.

l — Top start; slant down and a monkey tail.

m — Middle start; slant down, up over the hill, up over the hill again, and a monkey tail.

n — Middle start; slant down, up over the hill, and a monkey tail.

o — Middle start; around down and close up.

p — Middle start; slant down under water, up, around, and a tummy.

q — Middle start; around down, close up, down under water, and a backward fishhook.

r — Middle start; slant down, up, and a roof.

s — Start below the middle; curve up, around, down, and a snake tail.

t — Top start; slant down and a monkey tail. Cross.

u — Middle start; down, around, up, down, and a monkey tail.

v — Middle start; slant down right and slant up right.

w — Middle start; down, around, up, and down, around, up again.

x — Middle start; slant down right, and a monkey tail. Cross down left.

y — Middle start; down, around, up, down under water, and a fishhook.

z — Middle start; over right, slant down left, and over right.

Capital Letters

A — Top start; slant down left. Same start; slant down right. Middle bar across.

B — Top start; slant down, up, around halfway, close, around again, and close.

C — Start below the top; curve up, around, down, up, and stop.

D — Top start; slant down, up, around, and close.

E Top start; over left, slant down, and over right. Middle bar across.

F Top start; over left and slant down. Middle bar across.

G Start below the top, curve up, around, down, up, and over left.

H Top start; slant down. Another top start, to the right; slant down. Middle bar across.

I Top start; slant down. Cross the top and the bottom line.

J Top start; slant down and curve up left.

K Top start; slant down. Another top start, to the right; slant down left, touch, slant down right, and a monkey tail.

L Top start; slant down and over right.

M Top start; slant down. Same start; slant down right halfway, slant up right, and slant down.

N Top start; slant down. Same start; slant down right, and slant up.

O Top start; around down and close up.

P Top start; slant down, up, around halfway, and close.

Q Top start; around down and close up. Cross with a curve down right.

R Top start; slant down, up, around halfway, close, slant down right, and a monkey tail.

S Start below the top; curve up, around, down, and a snake tail.

T Top start; slant down. Cross the line at the top.

U Top start; slant down, around, up, down, and a monkey tail.

V Top start; slant down right and slant up right.

W Top start; slant down right, slant up right, slant down right, and slant up right again.

X Top start; slant down right and a monkey tail. Cross down left.

Y Top start; slant down right halfway. Another top start, to the right; slant down left, and touch on the way.

Z Top start; over right, slant down left, and over right.

Number Descriptions

1 Top start; slant down.

2 Start below the top; curve up, around, and slant down left, and over right.

3 Start below the top; curve up, around halfway; around again, up, and stop.

4 Top start; down halfway; over right. Another top start, to the right; slant down and through.

5 Top start; over left; slant down halfway; curve around, down, up, and stop.

6 Top start; slant down, and curve around; up, and close.

7 Top start; over right; slant down left.

8 Start below the top; curve up, around, down; a snake tail; slant up right; through, and touch.

9 Top start; curve down, around, close; slant down.

10 Top start; slant down. Another top start to the right; curve down, around, and close.

Cursive Letter Descriptions

Lower-case Letters

_a_ — Overhill; back, around down, close up, down, and up.

_b_ — Uphill high; loop down, around, up, and sidestroke.

_c_ — Overhill; back, around, down, and up.

_d_ — Overhill; back, around down, touch, up high, down, and up.

_e_ — Uphill; loop down, through, and up.

_f_ — Uphill high; loop down under water, loop up right, touch, and up.

_g_ — Overhill; back, around down, close up, down under water, loop up left, and through.

_h_ — Uphill high; loop down, up over the hill, and up.

_i_ — Uphill; down, and up. Add a dot.

_j_ — Uphill; down under water, loop up left, and through. Add a dot.

_k_ — Uphill high; loop down, up into a little tummy, slant down right, and up.

_l_ — Uphill high; loop down, and up.

_m_ — Overhill; down, up over the hill, up over the hill again, and up.

_n_ — Overhill; down, up over the hill, and up.

_o_ — Overhill; back, around down, close up, and sidestroke.

_p_ — Uphill; down under water, up, around into a tummy, and up.

_q_ — Overhill; back, around down, close up, down under water, loop up right, touch, and up.

_r_ — Uphill; sidestroke, down, and up.

_s_ — Uphill; down, around, close, and up.

_t_ — Uphill high; down, and up. Cross.

_u_ — Uphill; down, around, up, down, and up.

_v_ — Overhill; down, around, up, and sidestroke.

_w_ — Uphill; down, around, up, down, around, up again, and sidestroke.

_x_ — Overhill; slant down right, and up. Cross down left.

_y_ — Overhill; down, around, up, down under water, loop up left, and through.

_z_ — Overhill; around down, around again, and down under water, loop up left, and through.

Capital Letters

 Top start; around down, close up, down, and up.

 Top start; down, up, around halfway, around again, touch, sidestroke, and stop.

 Start below the top; curve up, around, down, and up.

 Top start; down, loop right, curve up, around, close, loop right, through, and stop.

 Start below the top; curve up, around to the middle, around again to the bottom line, and up.

 Start below the top; down, around, up, and sidestroke. Wavy cross and a straight cross.

 Bottom start; uphill high, loop through the middle, up, curve down, around, through the uphill, sidestroke, and stop.

 Start below the top; make a cane. Top start, to the right; down, up, left, touch, loop right, through, and stop.

 Start below the middle; sidestroke left, curve down, around, uphill high, loop down, and up.

 Bottom start; curve up, around, touch on the way down under water, loop up left, and through.

 Start below the top; make a cane. Top start, to the right; slant down left, touch, slant down right, and up.

 Start below the top; uphill, loop down, loop right, and up.

 Start below the top; make a cane, up over the hill, up over the hill again, and up.

 Start below the top; make a cane, up over the hill, and up.

 Top start; around down, close up, loop right, through, and stop.

 Top start; down, up, around halfway, and close.

 Start below the top; curve up, around, down, loop right, and up.

For an alternative way of writing cursive Q, see the stroke description for manuscript Q on page 9.

 Top start; down, up, around halfway, close, slant down right, and up.

 Bottom start; uphill high, loop through the middle, curve down, around, through the uphill, sidestroke, and stop.

 Start below the top; down, around, up, and sidestroke. Wavy cross.

 Start below the top; make a cane, around, up, down, and up.

 Start below the top; make a cane, around, slant up right, sidestroke, and stop.

 Start below the top; make a cane, around, up, down, around, up again, sidestroke, and stop.

 Start below the top; curve up, slant down right, and up. Cross down left.

 Start below the top; make a cane, around up, down under water, loop up left, and through.

Start below the top; curve up, around, down, around again, and down under water, loop up left, and through.

Reviewing Lower-case Manuscript Letters

Write the alphabet using manuscript letters.

a   b   c   d   e   f   g   h   i   j   k   l   m

n   o   p   q   r   s   t   u   v   w   x   y   z

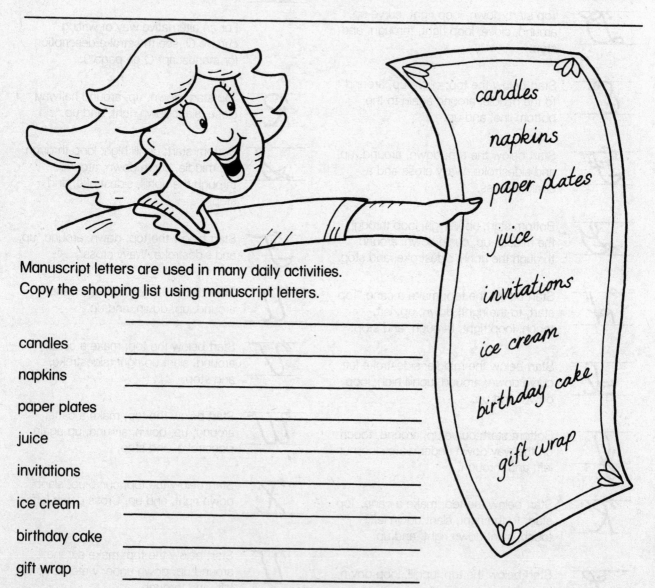

Manuscript letters are used in many daily activities.
Copy the shopping list using manuscript letters.

candles

napkins

paper plates

juice

invitations

ice cream

birthday cake

gift wrap

candles
napkins
paper plates
juice
invitations
ice cream
birthday cake
gift wrap

Check your writing. Are your letters formed correctly? Is the
space between the letters in the words even? Are the letters
the correct size?

© Scott Foresman - Addison Wesley

Name _____

Reviewing Capital Manuscript Letters

Capital letters are used for names of people, places, and
things. Use manuscript writing to label the planets. Write each
one with a capital letter.

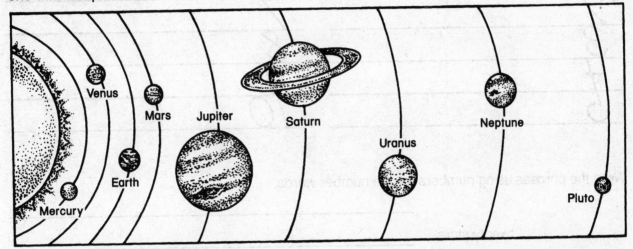

Mercury

_____

Venus

_____

Earth

_____

Mars

_____

Jupiter

_____

Saturn

_____

Uranus

_____

Neptune

_____

Pluto

_____

Write this caption for the diagram about the solar system. Use manuscript letters.

There are nine planets in the solar system.

_____

_____

Use these questions to evaluate your writing.

	Yes	No
Are the letters shaped correctly?	☐	☐
Are the letters the correct size?	☐	☐
Are the spaces between the letters in each word even?	☐	

© Scott Foresman - Addison Wesley

Reviewing Numbers

Write a row of each number.

1

2

3

4

5

6

7

8

9

0

Write the phrases using numbers for the number words.

twenty stars _____

ninety-two degrees _____

sixteen satellites _____

seventy-eight rings _____

one sun _____

nine planets _____

two hundred comets _____

twelve moons _____

© Scott Foresman - Addison Wesley

Practicing Cursive lL, hH, and kK

Write a row of each letter.

✏️ **Tips:** Make each letter go all the way to the top line. Keep the loops open.

l	*l*
h	*h*
k	*k*

✏️ **Tip:** Notice that **L** has two loops, **H** has one loop, and **K** has no loops.

L	*L*
H	*H*
K	*K*

Capital Letter Connections

Trace the letters in the boxes.

Remember that **L** and **K** join the letters that follow them.

H does not join the letter that follows it.

Le Ka

Hi

Write the following place names.

Kiowa   Louisville, Kentucky

Honolulu   Harahan, Louisiana

© Scott Foresman - Addison Wesley

Writing Cursive lL, hH, and kK

Write a row of each pair of letters.

Connections Tips: Curve up and back when connecting **lo**. Curve up and over for **ky**.
Curve up and loop back to connect **he**.

lo   *lo*

he   *he*

ky   *ky*

Write each sentence.

Legibility Tip: Leave even space between the letters in words.

Louisville, Kentucky, is located near the Ohio River.

Harahan, Louisiana, is close to the city of New Orleans.

Kiowa, Kansas, is north of the Oklahoma border.

Honolulu is near the Keehi Lagoon.

Where is your hometown?

© Scott Foresman - Addison Wesley

Practicing Cursive tT, iI, and uU

Write a row of each letter.

✏️ **Tips:** Make **i** and **u** half as tall as **t**. Cross **t** and dot **i**.

✏️ **Tips:** Cross **T** at the top line. Do not make **I** or **U** too wide.

Capital Letter Connections

Trace the letters in the boxes.

Remember that **I** and **U** join the letters that follow them.

T does not join the letter that follows it.

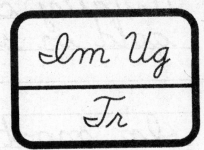

Write the following names of countries and their currency.

India, rupee   Tunisia, dinar

United States, dollar

© Scott Foresman - Addison Wesley

Writing Cursive tT, iI, and uU

Write a row of each pair of letters.

✏ **Connections Tips:** For **to** curve up and back. For **in** curve up and over.

For **us** curve up to the same height as **u**, then down and back.

to   *to*
in   *in*
us   *us*

Write each sentence.

✏ **Legibility Tip:** Small lower-case letters should be half the height of capital letters.

Before coins were invented,
people used stones for money.

The first coins were made in
Turkey.

Usually coins were made of
gold or silver.

In most places today, paper
money is used.

© Scott Foresman - Addison Wesley

Practicing Cursive eE, jJ, and pP

Write a row of each letter.

✏️ **Tips:** Dot **j**. Keep the loop open in **e**.

e

j

p

e

j

p

✏️ **Tips:** Add no loops to **E** and **P**. Keep the loops open in the **J**.

E

J

P

E

J

P

Capital Letter Connections

Trace the letters in the boxes,

Remember that **E** and **J** join the letters that follow them.

P does not join the letter that follows it.

Ea Ju

Pr

Write the following names of North Pole explorers.

Robert Peary, American Explorer

Naomi Uemura of Japan

© Scott Foresman - Addison Wesley

Writing Cursive eE, jJ, and pP

Write a row of each pair of letters.

✎ **Connections Tips:** Curve up and back to join **ea** and **jo**.
Curve all the way up to the top line to join **pl**.

ea

jo

pl

ea

jo

pl

Write each sentence.

✎ **Legibility Tip:** Make sure you slant all your letters in the same direction.

In 1909, Robert Peary reached the North Pole.

Exploring with him was Matthew Henson, an African American.

A Japanese explorer traveled alone to the pole.

Naomi Uemura had quite a job getting there by dog sled.

© Scott Foresman - Addison Wesley

Name _____

Practicing Cursive aA, dD, and cC

Write a row of each letter.

Tips: Close a and d. Keep c open.

a _____ *a*

d _____ *d*

c _____ *c*

Tips: Be sure **A** and **C** touch the bottom line. Be sure the **D** is closed at the top.

A _____ *A*

D _____ *D*

C _____ *C*

Capital Letter Connections

Trace the letters in the boxes.
Remember that **A** and **C** join the letters that follow them.
D does not join the letter that follows it.

Am Cr

Da

Write the following names of mathematicians.

Archimedes   *René Descartes*

Charles Babbage   *Copernicus*

© Scott Foresman - Addison Wesley

Name _____

Writing Cursive aA, dD, and cC

Write a row of each pair of letters.

✏ **Connections Tips:** Curve up and form a loop when connecting **ab** and **de**.
Curve up and back to make the connection for **co**.

ab   *ab*
de   *de*
co   *co*

Write each sentence.

✏ **Legibility Tip:** Make sure tall lower-case letters touch the top line.

Ancient Egyptians used decimals and geometry.

An Arab scholar wrote a book about algebra.

The Chinese used an abacus to solve problems.

Charles Babbage developed an early computer.

© Scott Foresman - Addison Wesley

Name _____

Review

Write these names and sentences in cursive.

⭐ **Remember:** The capital letters **A**, **C**, and **E** join the letters that follow them.

Agra _____

_____

Eiffel Tower _____

_____

Chartres _____

_____

⭐ **Remember:** The capital letters **P** and **T** do not join the letters that follows them.

Parthenon _____

_____

Taj Mahal _____

_____

Paris _____

_____

Notre Dame Cathedral has huge stained-glass windows.

_____

_____

Windsor Castle, outside of London, is the home of royalty.

_____

_____

Historic buildings face the Plaza de Armas in Lima, Peru.

_____

_____

Hagia Sophia has a huge dome and richly decorated interior.

_____

_____

© Scott Foresman - Addison Wesley

Evaluation

Write the paragraph below in cursive.
Use your best handwriting.

Remember: Keep the loops open in **e**, **h**, **j**, **k**, and **l**. Make sure the small letters are half the size of tall letters.

The Eiffel Tower is a famous landmark in Paris. The tower was built for the Universal Exposition in 1889. Alexandre Gustave Eiffel, an engineer, built the tower to show how iron and steel could be used to erect tall structures. The Eiffel Tower stands in a park called the Champ de Mars.

_____
_____
_____
_____
_____
_____
_____
_____

✓ **Check Your Handwriting**

	Yes	No
Are the loops open in **e**, **h**, **j**, **k**, and l?	☐	☐
Are the small letters half the size of tall letters?	☐	☐

© Scott Foresman - Addison Wesley

Practicing Cursive nN, mM, and xX

Write a row of each lower-case letter.

✎ **Tips:** Make **n**, **m**, and **x** the same height. Cross the **x** after writing the entire word.

Write a row of each capital letter.

✎ **Tips:** Put the correct number of curves in **N** and **M**. Cross the **X**.

Capital Letter Connections

Trace the letters in the boxes.

Remember that **N** and **M** join the letters that follow them.

X does not join the letter that follows it.

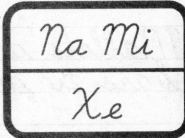

Write the following names for music shops.

Xavier's Xylophone Store

Nick's Shop for Musicians

© Scott Foresman - Addison Wesley

Name _____

Writing Cursive nN, mM, and xX

Write a row of each pair of letters.

✏ **Connections Tips:** To join **ng** and **ma** start at the bottom line. Curve up and back.
To join **xy** start at the bottom line. Curve up and over.

ng   *ng*

ma   *ma*

xy   *xy*

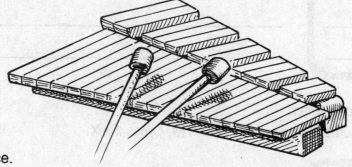

Write each sentence.

✏ **Legibility Tip:** Make sure your letters do not overlap, or bump into each other.

Xylophones have bars arranged like the keys of a piano.

Mallets are used to strike the bars to make sounds.

No one knows where or when the xylophone originated.

26

© Scott Foresman - Addison Wesley

Practicing Cursive gG, yY, and qQ

Write a row of each letter.

Tips: Swing the bottom loop of **g** and **y** to the left. Swing the bottom loop of **q** to the right.

Tip: Do not make the loops too big in **G**, **Y**, and **Q**.

Capital Letter Connections

Trace the letters in the boxes.

Remember that **Y** and **Q** join the letters that follow them.

G does not join the letter that follows it.

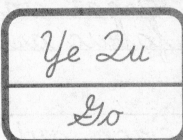

Write the following names of clubs.

Youngstown Quilting Club

Green Valley Quilters

© Scott Foresman - Addison Wesley

Writing Cursive gG, yY, and qQ

Write a row of each pair of letters.

Connections Tips: For **gn** and **yo** continue the loop of the **g** and **y** up to the top of the next letter. To connect **qu** bring the loop of the **q** up to the bottom line.

gn   gn
yo   yo
qu   qu

Write each sentence.

Legibility Tip: Use more space between words than between letters.

Young and old alike enjoy
quilting.

Quilters create exciting
designs.

Great varieties of colorful
fabric are required.

Each quilt is a work of art!

© Scott Foresman - Addison Wesley

Practicing Cursive oO, wW, and bB

Write a row of each lower-case letter.

✏️ **Tips:** Be sure o is closed. Keep the loop open in **b**.

o   *o*

w   *w*

b   *b*

Write a row of each capital letter.

✏️ **Tips:** Close **O**. Make both sides of **W** equal. Make the top and bottom of **B** the same.

O   *O*

W   *W*

B   *B*

Capital Letter Connections

Trace the letters in the box.

Remember that **O**, **W**, and **B** do not join the letters that follow them.

On Wh Bl

Write the following names of weather information groups.

World Weather Organization

Boston Weather Information

© Scott Foresman - Addison Wesley

Writing Cursive oO, wW, and bB

Write a row of each pair of letters.

✏ **Connections Tips:** When **o**, **w**, and **b** join to the next letter, the shape of the next letter changes. Notice that the connections begin in the middle of the space between the two lines, not at the bottom line.

ol   *ol*
wi   *wi*
be   *be*

Write each sentence.

✏ **Legibility Tip:** Make sure your writing is not too heavy or too light.

Observation stations collect weather information.

Wind vanes show the direction of the wind.

Barometers measure air pressure.

Satellites beam cloud pictures back to earth.

© Scott Foresman - Addison Wesley

Practicing Cursive vV and zZ

Write a row of each lower-case letter.

✏️ **Tips:** Make v touch the bottom line. Put only one loop in **z**.

v

z

Write a row of each capital letter.

✏️ **Tips:** Do not make V too wide. Use only one loop in **Z**.

V

Z

Capital Letter Connections

Trace the letters in the boxes.

Remember that **Z** joins the letter that follows it.

V does not join the letter that follows it.

Ze
Vo

Write the following Native American place names.

Village of the Zapotec

Village of the Zamuco

© Scott Foresman - Addison Wesley

Writing Cursive vV and zZ

Write a row of each pair of letters.

✏️ **Connections Tips:** When **v** joins to **e** and **z** joins to **i**, the shape of **e** and **i** change.

To join **zo** continue the loop up, over, and back.

ve   *ve*
zi   *zi*
zo   *zo*

Write each sentence.

✏️ **Legibility Tip:** Make small lower-case letters half the height of tall lower-case letters.

The Zuni are descendants
of the Anasazi.

They live near the Arizona
border.

Vast numbers of Zuni are
farmers.

The Zuni are known for their
native jewelry.

© Scott Foresman - Addison Wesley

Practicing Cursive sS, rR, and fF

Write a row of each letter.

✏️ **Tips:** Keep **r** open. Close **s**.

_s_   _s_

_r_   _r_

_f_   _f_

✏️ **Tips:** Do not make the loops in **S** and **R** too big. Remember to cross the **F**.

_S_   _S_

_R_   _R_

_F_   _F_

Capital Letter Connections

Trace the letters in the boxes.
Remember that **R** joins the letter that follows it.
S and **F** do not join the letters that follow them.

_Ra_

_Sh Fl_

Write the following names of fire departments.

Fremont Fire Squad

Roselle Fire Department

© Scott Foresman · Addison Wesley

Writing Cursive sS, rR, and fF

Write a row of each pair of letters.

✏️ **Connections Tips:** To join **sc** curve up, over, and back.
When joining **re** and **fi** curve up.

sc   *sc*

re   *re*

fi   *fi*

Write each sentence.

✏️ **Legibility Tip:** Keep you pencil moving. Do not draw your letters.

Firefighters are an important group in a community.

Captain Robins often visits our school.

She came during Fire Prevention Week.

Supervising school fire drills is one reason for her visits.

© Scott Foresman - Addison Wesley

Review

Write these names and sentences in cursive.

⭐ **Remember:** The capital letters **M**, **Y**, and **Z** join the letters that follow them.

Morse

Yale

Zeppelin

⭐ **Remember:** The capital letters **B**, **F**, and **S** do not join the letters that follow them.

Birdseye

Fulton

Salk

A Scottish blacksmith named Macmillan made the first bicycle.

Fires were easy to start after John Walker invented matches.

Ralph Baer invented "Odyssey," the first home video game.

Joseph Glidden built the first machine to make barbed wire.

© Scott Foresman - Addison Wesley

Evaluation

Write the paragraph below in cursive.
Use your best handwriting.

Remember: Make the loops of **g** and **y** the same length below the line. Use even spacing between words.

In 1893, Whitcomb Judson patented a shoe fastener that used hooks, eyes, and a slide fastener. This was one of the first zippers. Gideon Sunback patented a fastener with teeth that meshed. The B. F. Goodrich Company gave the name Zipper to galoshes with slide fasteners in 1923.

_____

_____

_____

_____

_____

_____

_____

_____

_____

_____

✔ **Check Your Handwriting**

	Yes	No
Are the loops of **g** and **y** the same length below the line?	☐	☐
Is there even spacing between words?	☐	☐

© Scott Foresman - Addison Wesley

Size and Proportion

Cursive lower-case letters can be small, can be tall, or can have descenders.
Small letters sit on the bottom line and are half a line tall.
These are small lower-case letters.

a c e i m n o r s u v w x

Choose three small lower-case letters that are most difficult for you to write and write them.

Tall letters extend from the bottom line to the top line.
These are the tall lower-case letters.

b d h k l t

Choose three tall lower-case letters that are your favorites and write them.

Descenders of letters extend half a line below the bottom line.
These are the lower-case letters with descenders.

f g j p q y z

Write three lower-case letters with descenders that you think are fun to write.

Watch the proportion of your handwriting. Capital letters should be twice the size of small letters.

Donald McCully

Write your first and last name. Concentrate on making letters the correct size.

Write the first and last name of a friend.

© Scott Foresman - Addison Wesley

Slant

How do you slant your writing? Write this sentence.

What will the weather be?

_____

_____

Look at these ways to slant handwriting. Compare
them with your sentence above. Write the word that
describes the slant of your handwriting.

left

left

right

right

straight

straight

Write each sentence. Use the slant you are most comfortable
with, but remember to slant all your letters in the same direction.

A meteorologist forecasts the weather.

_____

_____

_____

Thermometers are used to measure temperature.

_____

_____

_____

Air pressure is measured with a barometer.

_____

_____

© Scott Foresman - Addison Wesley

Name _____

Letter, Word, and Sentence Spacing

Spacing is important when you write. Notice what happens
when the spacing between letters is not even. Write the word
using even spacing between the letters.

camera

The space between words is larger than the space between
letters. The space is about the size of the tip of your pencil.
Study the model. Then write the phrase correctly.

film and flash

The space between sentences is larger than the space between words.
The space is about the size of the width of your pencil. Look at the
model. Then write the sentences, spacing them correctly.

Use the camera lens to focus the picture. Then the picture will be sharp and clear.

Write the sentences. Space your letters, words, and sentences evenly.

Photographs appear in magazines, billboards, books, and newspapers.
They show people, places, and events.

© Scott Foresman - Addison Wesley

Smoothness

Handwriting needs to be easy to read. If the writing is too dark or too light or if the lines are wavy or jagged, the writing will be difficult to read.

This writing is either too dark or too light. Write the phrase using the correct line weight.

photo album   *photo album*

Form your letters with a smooth, continuous stroke. Keep your pencil moving. Try not to draw your letters. This will help keep your writing from becoming wavy or jagged. Write the phrase so the words are smooth and even.

happy family memories

Write the sentences. Keep your handwriting smooth and even. Be sure your line weight is not too dark or too light.

Neil visited his grandparents during summer vacation.
They took a ferry across Lake Michigan.

© Scott Foresman - Addison Wesley

Name _____

Closing Letters

If letters are not formed correctly, words become difficult to read. Look at the words below. Can you tell what they are? Why are they difficult to read?

purl   *flrit*

Did you figure out that the words above are *pool* and *float?* They are difficult to read because the round letters **p, o,** and **a** were not closed. These letters must be closed when they are written. If they are not closed, the handwriting becomes difficult to read.

Here are the round letters. Remember to close them. Practice writing each letter.

a   d   g   o   p   q   s

Some capital letters are also round letters. Keep them closed just like you do the lower-case letters. Practice these capitals.

a   O   P   R

Write the sentences. Remember to close your round letters.

Allen practiced a new dive. Paula worked on her backstroke.
Orin and Roberta did the sidestroke down the length of the pool.

© Scott Foresman - Addison Wesley

Keeping Loops in Letters

Here is a mystery for you to solve. What does the phrase below say?
Can you figure out why it is so difficult to read?

length of the field

The mystery phrase is *length of the field*. It is hard to read because
the loops in the letters **l**, **e**, **g**, **h**, and **f** were not kept open.

All these words need loops in some of their letters. Write the words. Use loops.

field

_____

players

_____

helmet

_____

zero

_____

Write the sentences. Remember to keep the loops in your letters open.

The length of a lacrosse field is 110 yards. The goals are 6 feet high
and 6 feet wide. A center line divides the field in half. A solid rubber
ball and sticks with nets are used.

_____

_____

_____

_____

_____

© Scott Foresman - Addison Wesley

Avoiding Loops in Letters

Sometimes extra loops are added to letters. When this happens, some words are difficult to read. Look at the phrase below. It says *first-aid kit*. Notice how loops have been added to the three **i**'s, the two **t**'s, and the **d**.

first-aed ket

Do not add loops to the letters below. Practice writing them correctly.

d   i   m   m   n   p   t   u   w

Rewrite this list of things to include in a first-aid kit. Remember not to add loops.

bandages

bandages

antiseptic

anteseptec

tweezers

teveezers

© Scott Foresman - Addison Wesley

Keeping Round Strokes Round

Look at the round strokes below. Notice how some letters have
a rounded curve at the top and some letters have a rounded
curve at the bottom. Practice writing the letters.

m   n   u   v   w   y

Notice what happens when the rounded curves are turned into
sharp points. Write the words correctly.

fault

fault

waves

waves

mountains

mountains

Write the sentences. Keep round strokes round.

When the earth shakes, it is called an earthquake. Usually
earthquakes begin along fault lines. A seismograph measures
the earth's motion during an earthquake.

© Scott Foresman - Addison Wesley

Review

Check the box that tells how to correct each word. Write the word correctly. Then write the sentence at the bottom of the page. Try to avoid the handwriting mistakes you see on the page.

elements   *ilimints*   _____

☐ Keep the loops open.   ☐ Make the letters taller.

oxygen   *oxygen*   _____

☐ Make the writing less jagged.   ☐ Space the letters evenly.

copper   *copper*   _____

☐ Add a loop to e.   ☐ Slant letters in the same direction.

helium   *helium*   _____

☐ Use the correct letter size.   ☐ Make the writing less dark.

silver   *silver*   _____

☐ Make letters taller.   ☐ Space the letters evenly.

O   Cu   He   Ag
Oxygen   Copper   Helium   Silver

Chemical symbols are a shorthand way of representing the names of the elements.

_____

_____

_____

_____

© Scott Foresman - Addison Wesley

Evaluation

Write the paragraph below in cursive.
Use your best handwriting.

Remember: Watch the shape, size, slant, smoothness, and spacing of your letters, words, and sentences.

Elements are all around us. Soda cans are made from aluminum. Silicon chips are used in computers. Jewelry is fashioned from silver, gold, and copper. The striking surface of a match is made from a combination of sand and red phosphorus. Zinc is used in electric batteries.

_____

_____

_____

_____

_____

_____

_____

_____

_____

✓ **Check Your Handwriting**

	Yes	No
Are letters shaped correctly?	☐	☐
Are tall lower-case and small lower-case letters the correct size?	☐	☐
Do all letters slant in the same direction?	☐	☐
Is the writing smooth and even?	☐	☐
Is there even spacing between letters, words, and sentences?	☐	☐

© Scott Foresman - Addison Wesley

Connecting l, i, and q

The letters **l**, **i**, and **q** end with an uphill stroke. The letters **e**, **r**, and **u** begin with an uphill stroke. Connect the letters at the bottom line. Make sure the tall letters touch the top line and the small letters are half as tall. Write the connections.

le   *le*

ir   *ir*

qu   *qu*

Write the words and sentences below.

trees   *squirrel*   *birds*

evergreen   *maples*   *peaceful*

A forest provides a home for many birds

The autumn leaves are quite colorful.

© Scott Foresman - Addison Wesley

Connecting s, p, and e

Look at the pairs of letters. Notice that they connect at the
bottom line. When writing these letter pairs, make sure they are
not too close together or too far apart. Write the connections.

sh   *sh*
pr   *pr*
er   *er*

Write the words and sentences below.

flower   *rabbit*   *deer*

nests   *shade*   *springs*

*The wolf searches the fields
and forest for prey.*

Bears hunt for berry bushes.

© Scott Foresman - Addison Wesley

Name _____

Connecting c, h, and r

The letters **c**, **h**, and **r** end with an uphill stroke. The letters **a** and **o** begin with an overhill stroke. Curve up and over to make these connections. Be sure to keep the rounded strokes in **a** and **o** closed. Write the connections.

ca   *ca*
ho   *ho*
ra   *ra*

Write the words and sentences below.

home   *rain*

temperature   *climate*

world   *landscape*

The hot, dry desert is a harsh environment.

The desert can get very cold at night.

© Scott Foresman - Addison Wesley

Connecting a, n, and u

Look at the pairs of letters. Notice that they connect at the bottom line. When writing these pairs of letters, be sure that you slant both letters in the same direction. Write the connections.

an   *an*

nd   *nd*

un   *un*

Write the words and sentences below.

lizard   *sand*   *cactus*

plants   *dune*   *mesa*

Many kinds of snakes live in the American deserts.

Some desert animals live underground to keep cool.

© Scott Foresman - Addison Wesley

Name _____

Connecting y, z, and g

The letters **y**, **z**, and **g** end with an overhill stroke. The letters **e**, **u**, and **r** begin with an uphill stroke. When you connect the letters, be sure to space them correctly. Do not make the letters too close or too far apart. Write the connections.

ye   *ye*

zu   *zu*

gr   *gr*

California

Write the words and sentences below.

ground   *jeopardy*   *damage*

geology   *fright*   *zero*

California has quite a few earthquakes each year.

A major fault lies just along the coast.

© Scott Foresman - Addison Wesley

Connecting g, y, and j

Look at the pairs of letters. Notice that they connect at the bottom line. When you write these letters, be sure that the small letters are half the height of the tall letters. Write the connections.

gh   *gh*
yo   *yo*
ji   *ji*

Write the words and sentences below.

buildings   *jolt*   *night*

signs   *edgy*   *jittery*

An earthquake's strength is measured on the Richter scale.

Would you be frightened if the earth moved?

© Scott Foresman · Addison Wesley

Connecting t, k, and m

The letters **t**, **k**, and **m** end with an uphill stroke. Notice that they connect with the next letter at the bottom line. When writing these pairs of letters, be sure to write each letter the correct size. Write the connections.

th

ke

ma

th

ke

ma

Write the words and sentences below.

tropical

climate

windy

weather

cloudy

map

Tornadoes and hurricanes can strike in the United States.

Distant thunder may signal an approaching storm.

© Scott Foresman - Addison Wesley

Name

Connecting d, x, and f

Look at the pairs of letters. When writing these pairs of letters, connect them at the bottom line. Be sure **d** and **f** touch the top line. Write the connections.

dr   dr

xp   xp

fr   fr

Write the words and sentences below.

cold   dry   drizzle

foggy   icy   moisture

Some parts of the country have rainy winters.

Does your area experience snow and freezing rain?

© Scott Foresman - Addison Wesley

Name

Review

Write the connections, words, and sentences in cursive.

⭐ **Remember:** Curve up and loop back to make these connections.

th   ie   al   ch   pl

math   equal   multiply

⭐ **Remember:** Curve up and over to make these connections.

ea   to   ig   em   yo

total   problem   digit

π ✕ ÷ ± ✕ ÷ ∞ ÷ + = > π ✕ ÷ ± ✕ ÷ ∞ ÷

In math, multiply to find the product.

The total in addition is called the sum.

A division problem may have a remainder.

© Scott Foresman - Addison Wesley

Name _____

Evaluation

Write the paragraph below in cursive.
Use your best handwriting.

Remember: Keep loops open in the letters l, **h**, and **e**. Be sure tall letters touch the top line.

Kim and Ray made a trip to the grocery store. They got two pounds of grapes for $1.18 a pound, chicken for $5.27, plus hot sauce for $1.69. When checking out, they presented coupons worth 70¢. The tax was 64¢. They divided the cost between them. How much did each pay?

_____

_____

_____

_____

_____

_____

_____

_____

_____

✓ **Check Your Handwriting**

	Yes	No
Are loops open in the letters l, **h**, and **e**?	☐	☐
Do tall letters touch the top line?	☐	☐

Did you get an answer of $4.63?

© Scott Foresman - Addison Wesley

Connecting b

The letter **b** ends with a sidestroke. Look at the letters **l**, **a**, and **i**. When you connect **b** to these letters, the shape of the second letter changes. Keep the spacing between the letters even. Write the connections.

bl   *bl*
ba   *ba*
bi   *bi*

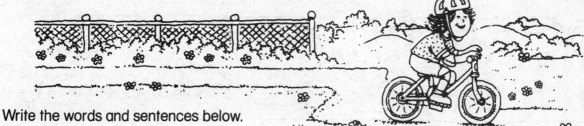

Write the words and sentences below.

habit   *automobiles*

basket   *handlebars*

visible   *brakes*

Everyone should learn the basics of bicycle safety.

Always wear a helmet when you ride a bicycle.

© Scott Foresman - Addison Wesley

Name _____

Connecting w

Look at the pairs of letters. When you connect **w** with another letter, the shape of the second letter changes. Study the way the second letter in each connection was changed. When you write the connections, be sure that each letter is the correct size. Write the connections.

wh   *wh*

wa   *wa*

wi   *wi*

Write the words and sentences below.

water   *swimmer*   *waves*

wise   *watching*   *wind*

You should never go swimming alone.

Don't horse around when in a pool.

© Scott Foresman - Addison Wesley

Connecting o

The letter **o** ends with a sidestroke. Look at the letter after each **o**.
You connect them halfway between the top and bottom line. Be sure
to change the shape of the second letter. Write the connections.

ob   *ob*

on   *on*

oo   *oo*

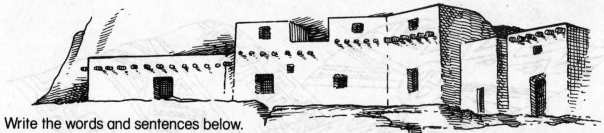

Write the words and sentences below.

Southwest   *ceremony*

town   *woven*

pots   *tools*

*The Pueblo Indians built
adobe dwellings.*

*Their main foods were corn
and beans.*

© Scott Foresman - Addison Wesley

Connecting v

Look at the pairs of letters. Notice that **v** connects to the next letter between the top and bottom line. When writing each letter pair, be sure the letters slant in the same direction. Write the connections.

va _____ *va*

ve _____ *ve*

vi _____ *vi*

Write the words and sentences below.

weave   *silver*   *variety*

vivid   *festival*   *village*

The Navajo lived in hogans, houses covered with mud.

They have made blankets for centuries.

© Scott Foresman - Addison Wesley

Name _____

Connecting b, o, and w

The letters **b**, **o**, and **w** end with a sidestroke. When you
connect these letters, the shape of the second letter changes.
Be sure to keep **o** closed. Write the connections.

bo _____ *bo*

oo _____ *oo*

wo _____ *wo*

Write the words and sentences below.

hoop _____ *coach* _____

professional _____ *bounce* _____

won _____ *turnover* _____

*Basketball was invented in
Massachusetts in 1891.*

*The basketball goals were
made out of peach baskets.*

© Scott Foresman - Addison Wesley

Connecting b, o, and v

Look at the pairs of letters. Notice that they do not join at the bottom line. They join between the top and bottom line. When writing these pairs of letters, be sure to use even spacing. Write the connections.

ba _____ *ba*

oa _____ *oa*

vo _____ *vo*

Write the words and sentences below.

goal _____ *ball* _____ *champion*

save _____ *forward* _____ *volley*

Soccer is the most popular sport in the world.

It is known as football in many countries.

© Scott Foresman - Addison Wesley

Name _____

Review

Write the connections, words, and sentences in cursive.

⭐ **Remember:** Some letters do not join at the bottom. When letters join in the space between the two lines, the shape of the second letter changes.

ow   be   va   on   we

_____

_____

vi   bo   wh   oz   or

_____

_____

region   northern   weather

_____

_____

caribou   berries   frozen

_____

_____

The Arctic region has many natural resources.

_____

_____

_____

The land is frozen in winter, but flowers bloom in spring.

_____

_____

_____

Animals such as foxes and caribou live on the tundra.

_____

_____

_____

© Scott Foresman - Addison Wesley

Name _____

Evaluation

Write the paragraph below in cursive.
Use your best handwriting.

Remember: Change the shape of letters that follow **b**, **o**, **v**, and **w**. Do not make letters too close or too far apart.

The Eskimos have lived in the Arctic for thousands of years. They adapted to their harsh climate by wearing animal skins. They built houses of ice when they traveled. They hunted polar bears and whales and caught fish. Now they have modern fishing boats and drive snowmobiles.

_____

_____

_____

_____

_____

_____

_____

_____

✓ **Check Your Handwriting**   Yes   No

Did you change the shape of letters that follow **b**, **o**, **v**, and **w**?   ☐   ☐

Are your letters not too close and not too far apart?   ☐   ☐

© Scott Foresman - Addison Wesley

Name _____

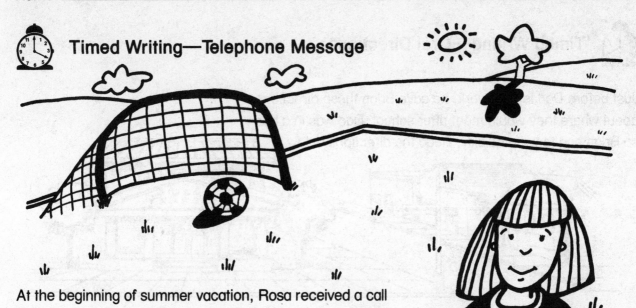

Timed Writing—Telephone Message

At the beginning of summer vacation, Rosa received a call from her soccer coach. Read what the coach said to Rosa.

Hi, Rosa, this is Katerina from the park district. I'm calling all the soccer players to tell them that practice starts on Monday, June 5. We'll practice every Monday, Wednesday, and Friday morning from 9:30 to 11:00. This year all soccer practice and games will be held at the new soccer field in Kennedy Park. If you need to call me, my number is 555-3737. Any questions?

Use these tips to help you take a telephone message.
- Ask the caller to wait until you get a pencil and paper.
- Write important information such as name, date, time, and place. Use manuscript or cursive handwriting, whichever is faster.
- Ask the caller to repeat information that you are not sure of.

Write the message from Katerina in the space below. Time your writing. Use a clock or a timer, or have a friend time you. Stop writing when four minutes are up.

Now read what you wrote. Did you write the dates, times, and numbers correctly?

© Scott Foresman - Addison Wesley

Name _____

 Timed Writing—Oral Directions

Just before Dad left for work, he gave Brian these directions
about where they would meet after school. Dad was in a hurry,
so Brian had to write quickly. Read the directions below.

    After leaving the school building, walk to the corner.
That's the corner of Fifth Avenue and Elm Street. Turn
left on Elm. Walk for three blocks until you reach Oak
Street. Turn right and go one block to Trail Road. Cross
Trail Road at the traffic light, and you'll end up at the
front door of the Main Library. Wait inside the front door,
and we'll go to the book sale together.

Use these tips when someone gives you directions.
• Use manuscript or cursive handwriting, whichever is faster
  for you to write.
• Write down the important names and numbers.
• Ask the person to repeat anything you are not sure of.

Imagine that you are Brian. Write the directions in the space
below. Time your writing. Use a clock or a timer, or have a
friend time you. Stop when four minutes are up.

_____

_____

_____

_____

_____

Now read what you wrote. Could you follow the directions?
Did you write the names and numbers clearly?

© Scott Foresman - Addison Wesley

Name _____

Have you ever read a textbook chapter and then forgot what you read? If you take short notes, you will probably remember more.

Use these tips to take notes from a textbook.
- First read through the part you are assigned.
- Go back and write down important facts, dates, and definitions. Use manuscript or cursive handwriting, whichever you write faster.
- Write legibly so that you can read the notes at a later time.

Read the paragraph about the Statue of Liberty. In the space below, write three or four notes about what you read. Time your reading and note-taking. Use a clock or a timer, or have a friend time you. Stop when four minutes are up.

   The Statue of Liberty is one of the most recognizable American monuments. The people of France gave the statue to the United States. It was a gift to celebrate the friendship between the two countries and the 100th birthday of the United States in 1876. The statue was so large that it had to be disassembled in France and then rebuilt in New York City. It arrived in New York in 1885. It was placed on Bedloe's Island in New York Harbor a year later. Bedloe's Island later became Liberty Island, a fitting name for the statue's home. More than one million people visit the statue each year.

_____

_____

_____

_____

_____

_____

Can you understand what you wrote? Did you write important facts, dates, and names?

© Scott Foresman - Addison Wesley

Name _____

Timed Writing—Oral Message

Roberto heard this message on the car radio. As soon as he got home, he wrote it down to give to his father. Read what he heard.

"Rush down to Sun's Saving Store! We are having a wonderful Back-to-School Sale. Buy pens, pencils, crayons, tablets, and notebooks. Today and tomorrow, everything here costs twenty cents, or buy three things for fifty cents. Come to 66 South Street. Look for the big yellow sun in the front. We will give you a yellow pencil free if you say the secret words "Savings at Sun." Remember the sale is Monday and Tuesday.

Use these tips when you write a message for someone else.
- Include important names, dates, and events.
- Use manuscript or cursive handwriting, whichever is faster.
- Write in complete sentences so that the message will be easy for the reader to understand.

Decide what parts of the radio message are important to write down. Then write the message in the space below. Time your writing. Use a clock or a timer, or have a friend time you. Stop when four minutes are up.

_____
_____
_____
_____

Now read what you wrote. Did you write down the names, days, and events?

© Scott Foresman - Addison Wesley

Name _____

Pronoun-Verb Agreement

> The pronouns **I**, **you**, **he**, **she**, **it**, **we**, and **they** are used in the subject of a sentence and must agree with the verb.

Incorrect: Andrea and <u>her</u> went swimming.
Correct: Andrea and <u>she</u> went swimming.

Incorrect: <u>Him and me</u> took a trip.
Correct: <u>He and I</u> took a trip.

Rewrite each sentence. Replace each underlined word with the correct pronoun. Remember to use even spacing between words.

1. Grandma and <u>Brian</u> make jelly.

_____

_____

2. Dad and <u>the twins</u> play basketball in the park on Saturdays.

_____

_____

3. Uncle Pedro and <u>Maria</u> sing duets in Spanish.

_____

_____

4. My sister and <u>me</u> tell each other secrets.

_____

_____

5. Mom and <u>him</u> enjoy visiting the art museum.

_____

_____

© Scott Foresman - Addison Wesley

Capitalizing Proper Nouns

> Capitalize the names of people, places, and pets.

Nancy Kwan	Tiger	Comstock, California
Uncle Tony	Rover	El Paso, Texas
the Williams family	Fluffy	Coral Gables, Florida

Write a proper noun for each person or place.

1. a relative

_____

_____

2. a friend

_____

_____

3. a state

_____

_____

4. a country

_____

_____

Rewrite each sentence. Add capital letters where they are needed.
Be sure to form the capital letters carefully and correctly.

5. My name is gina baxter.

_____

_____

6. My family lives in salem, oregon, on oak street.

_____

_____

_____

7. Last summer we traveled to yosemite national park.

_____

_____

_____

8. We met danny and carla gordon from canada on a hiking trail there.

_____

_____

_____

© Scott Foresman - Addison Wesley

Name _____

Using Vivid Details

Use vivid details to create a picture in the reader's mind. One way to create vivid details is to use strong verbs and colorful adjectives.

Write a strong verb or a colorful adjective for each word below.

Strong Verbs		Colorful Adjectives

1. ran _____
2. jumped _____
3. said _____
4. walked _____
5. saw _____

6. pretty _____
7. big _____
8. little _____
9. sad _____
10. happy _____

Rewrite each sentence. Use vivid details to create a picture in a reader's mind. Make sure to slant all letters in the same direction.

11. I ran to the telephone when it rang.

_____

_____

_____

12. Would I feel happy or sad when I heard the news?

_____

_____

_____

13. I saw my hand trembling as I reached for the receiver.

_____

_____

_____

© Scott Foresman - Addison Wesley

A Personal Narrative

When you write about something that happened to you or something you did, you are writing a personal narrative.

Read the personal narrative. Mark the errors that need to be corrected. Find one missing capital letter, two incorrect pronouns, and one misspelled word.

☰	Make a capital.
/	Make a small letter.
∧	Add something.
ℒ	Take out something.
⊙	Add a period.
¶	New paragraph.

There was a bear! It lumbered along, sniffing the grund. After james and I reeled in our fishing lines, him and I quietly backed away from the stream. James and me were relieved to have escaped unharmed.

Writing Tip: Use words that paint a vivid picture.

Write about something that happened to you or something you did. Tell how you felt about the experience. Keep your pencil moving. Do not draw your letters.

_____

_____

_____

_____

_____

_____

_____

_____

© Scott Foresman · Addison Wesley

Name _____

Adjectives in Comparisons

> When you compare one thing with another, you use adjectives. Use the ending *-er* to compare two things and the ending *-est* to compare more than two things.

Incorrect: Mt. Jackson is the <u>highest</u> of the two peaks.
Correct: Mt. Jackson is the <u>higher</u> of the two peaks.

Rewrite each sentence. Use the correct form of the adjective in parentheses. When writing *-er* and *-est,* watch the spacing between **e** and the next letter.

1. Lake Crystal is the (clear) lake in the entire country.

_____

_____

_____

2. The autumn leaves looked (bright) this year than last year.

_____

_____

_____

3. Of these three trees, the redwood is the (large).

_____

_____

_____

4. That was the (pretty) sunset I have ever seen.

_____

_____

_____

5. Of the two wildflowers, the primrose is the (rare).

_____

_____

_____

© Scott Foresman - Addison Wesley

Commas in a Series

> Use commas between series of words in a sentence.

The students grew peas, beans, and radishes in the class garden.
They used compost to make a rich, dark soil.

Rewrite the sentences. Use commas correctly. Remember to make lower-case letters half the height of capital letters.

1. Pete grew tomatoes lettuce and squash for the fair.

_____

_____

2. The winning tomato was big red and shiny.

_____

_____

_____

3. The fruit stand sold melons peaches and strawberries.

_____

_____

4. Allison made a sweet juicy pie.

_____

_____

5. The most popular pies were apple peach and blueberry.

_____

_____

© Scott Foresman - Addison Wesley

Name _____

Sensory Words

> Words that appeal to the senses will make your writing descriptive. Sensory words help the reader see, hear, feel, taste, or smell what you are describing.

The air felt <u>chilly</u> and <u>damp</u> on the soccer field.

Here are some sensory words. Add other sensory words to the chart.

See	Hear	Feel	Taste	Smell
shiny	squeaky	wet	salty	flowery
1. ____	3. ____	5. ____	7. ____	9. ____
2. ____	4. ____	6. ____	8. ____	10. ____

Rewrite each sentence. Add one or more sensory words for each blank. Be sure to close lower-case **a** and **d**.

11. The players' shirts looked ____ .

_____

_____

_____

12. The ground felt ____ as we ran toward the goal.

_____

_____

_____

13. The popcorn at the refreshment stand smelled ____ .

_____

_____

_____

14. I heard ____ voices as I scored the winning goal.

_____

_____

_____

© Scott Foresman - Addison Wesley

A Description

> When you appeal to the senses and help a reader see, hear, feel, taste, and smell a scene, you are writing a description.

☰	Make a capital.
/	Make a small letter.
∧	Add something.
ℒ	Take out something.
⊙	Add a period.
¶	New paragraph.

Read the description. Mark the errors that need to be corrected. Find two errors in adjectives used to compare and three errors in comma use.

Our trip to the city was greatest than any other trip we have taken. The city smelled like hot pavement and car fumes. The sun looked bright above stone, steel and glass buildings. Yet it was dark dim and cool on the street. Compared to our small town, the city was by far the noisiest. We heard honking horns and screaming sirens.

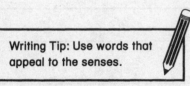

Writing Tip: Use words that appeal to the senses.

Describe a place you have been that had a lot of interesting sights, sounds, feelings, tastes, and smells. Use sensory words. Be sure your capital letters touch the top line.

_____

_____

_____

_____

_____

_____

_____

© Scott Foresman - Addison Wesley

Name _____

Subject-Verb Agreement

The subject and verb of a sentence must agree.

Incorrect: Homemade <u>pizza</u> **taste** great.
Correct: Homemade <u>pizza</u> **tastes** great.

Incorrect: <u>Tomato sauce and cheese</u> **is** important ingredients.
Correct: <u>Tomato sauce and cheese</u> **are** important ingredients.

Rewrite each sentence. Write the correct form of the verb. Do not crowd your letters when you are making connections. Use even spacing between letters.

1. Sometimes Tim and Shawna (cooks, cook) dinner.

_____

_____

2. Their recipe for tacos (is, are) great.

_____

_____

3. They (adds, add) a spicy sauce to ground beef.

_____

_____

4. The Harrises (eats, eat) spaghetti every Friday night.

_____

_____

5. Tamika always (make, makes) a salad to go with dinner.

_____

_____

© Scott Foresman - Addison Wesley

Name _____

Capitalizing and Punctuating Lists and Abbreviations

Abbreviations should be capitalized and followed by a period.

<u>Dr.</u> Janson   <u>Ms.</u> Chang   <u>Mrs.</u> Kennedy   <u>Mr.</u> Menendez

When writing a list, number it. Put a period after the number.
Capitalize the first letter of each item if it is a sentence.
End each sentence with a period.

How to Play "Crazy Eights"
1. Deal eight cards to each player.
2. Put the remaining cards in a pile between the players.

Rewrite each list item. Use correct punctuation and
capitalization. Remember to leave space between the
number and its period and the first word of the list.

Directions to Jim's House

1. go south on River Drive for three blocks

_____

_____

_____

2. when you see ms lazlo's mailbox, turn left

_____

_____

_____

3. go past mr and mrs Allen's white house

_____

_____

_____

4. don't park your bike on dr smith's driveway

_____

_____

_____

© Scott Foresman - Addison Wesley

Putting Directions in Correct Order

When you explain how to do something, be sure to write the directions in order, step by step. Use words like *first, then, next,* and *finally* to help make your directions clear.

Decide on the correct order for these steps in setting a table. Put a number beside each step to show its order.

_____ Put a fork between the plate and the napkin.

_____ First put a tablecloth or placemats on the table.

_____ Next put a napkin to the left of the plate.

_____ Finally, put a knife and spoon to the right of the plate.

_____ Put a plate down for each person.

Rewrite the steps in cleaning your room. Add words that help make the order of the steps clear. Make sure the bottom loops of the letters **f**, **g**, **j**, **p**, and **q** are open.

1. Sort the stuff on the floor and bed into piles.

_____

_____

_____

2. Put the stuff away in your closet, hamper, and drawers.

_____

_____

3. Make your bed.

_____

_____

4. Dust the furniture, and vacuum the floor.

_____

_____

© Scott Foresman - Addison Wesley

Name _____

Directions

Directions tell a reader how to do or make something.
Good directions are written in step-by-step order.

≡ Make a capital.
/ Make a small letter.
∧ Add something.
⌿ Take out something.
⊙ Add a period.
¶ New paragraph.

Read the directions. Mark the errors that need to be corrected.
Find one subject-verb agreement error, one punctuation error,
one capitalization error, and one misspelled word.

Mrs Feldman's Microwave Snack

1. First break a graham cracker in half.
2. put a marshmallow on one half of
   the cracker.
3. Next add a thin peice of chocolate bar.
4. Then put the other half of the cracker
   on top.
5. Finally, microwave until the chocolate
   and marshmallow melts.

Writing Tip: Write direc-tions in step-by-step order.

Write directions that tell your reader how to make a good
snack. Do not add loops to capital letters such as **B**, **E**, and **R**.

_____

_____

_____

_____

_____

_____

_____

_____

© Scott Foresman - Addison Wesley

© Scott Foresman - Addison Wesley

Name _____

Irregular Verbs

Some verbs have irregular forms. Sometimes these verbs are used with the helping verbs *has* and *have*. Use the helping verb *has* with singular subjects. Use the helping verb *have* with plural subjects.

Present	Past	Past with *has, have*
run, runs	ran	(has, have) run
see, sees	saw	(has, have) seen
go, goes	went	(has, have) gone

Incorrect: The lion <u>has became</u> mean and cruel.
Correct: The lion <u>has become</u> mean and cruel.

Rewrite each sentence. Use the correct verb forms.
Use a sidestroke to end v so it does not look like a u.

1. The rabbit and the fox (drank, drunk) water from the stream.

_____

_____

_____

2. The lion (seen, saw) the animals.

_____

_____

3. Other animals have (went, gone) to warn the rabbit and fox.

_____

_____

_____

4. Everyone has (become, became) frightened of the lion.

_____

_____

_____

5. The lion (forgotten, forgot) that kindness is better than cruelty.

_____

_____

_____

81

Quotation Marks

> Use quotation marks to show a speaker's exact words.
> Use a capital letter to begin the first word inside the
> quotation marks. Put a comma or the punctuation mark
> that ends the sentence before the final quotation mark.

"I am tired of running away from the lion," said the giraffe.
"What can we do?" asked the hippo.

Rewrite each sentence to show the speaker's exact words.
Make sure that the size of your writing is not too big or too small.

Example: We will have a meeting by the banana tree tomorrow
night. (giraffe)

"We will have a meeting by the banana tree tomorrow
night," announced the giraffe.

1. The banana tree is too far from my home. (antelope)

_____

_____

_____

2. Can we meet at the river? (hippo)

_____

_____

_____

3. The lion will see us in the moonlight. (parrot)

_____

_____

_____

4. We must try to agree. (elephant)

_____

_____

_____

5. We must work together to get things done. (monkey)

_____

_____

_____

© Scott Foresman - Addison Wesley

Name _____

Writing Dialogue

> When you show the exact words of a conversation between two or more characters, it is called a dialogue. Good dialogue shows the speaker's character traits. It makes a story vivid and lifelike.

When you write a dialogue, begin a new paragraph for each speaker.

"I am the strongest animal in the jungle," boasted the lion.

"You are a bully," whispered the mouse.

Rewrite the paragraph as a dialogue that shows the exact words of the speakers. Begin your capital letters far enough away from the quotation marks so that the capital letters do not touch them.

The antelope shouted that the animals should teach the lion a lesson. The monkey said he had read that those who act tough are often fearful. The parrot rudely asked what the monkey knew about being tough. The monkey said quietly that often the best lessons are learned from books.

_____

_____

_____

_____

_____

_____

_____

_____

© Scott Foresman - Addison Wesley

A Fable

When you write a very short story with animal characters and a moral, or lesson, at the end, you are writing a fable.

Read the fable. Mark the errors that need to be corrected.
Find one error in irregular verb use, one statement that needs quotation marks and end punctuation, and one new paragraph.

≡	Make a capital.
/	Make a small letter.
∧	Add something.
℮	Take out something.
⊙	Add a period.
¶	New paragraph.

The lion awoke suddenly in the middle
   of the night and sitted up.
"Who's there?" the lion asked nervously.
"Nobody," said the giraffe.
"It's only the moon," said the antelope. "Who's where?"
   asked the elephant.
Now you know how it feels to be afraid said the parrot.
"Next time put yourself in other people's shoes before you
   do something hurtful," said the monkey.

Writing Tip: Use dialogue
to help tell your story.

Write a fable. Create animal characters and end with a moral.
Remember to make your letters smooth and not shaky.

_____
_____
_____
_____
_____
_____
_____
_____

© Scott Foresman - Addison Wesley

Name _____

Adjectives in Comparisons

When you compare one thing to another, you use
adjectives. Add *-er* or *-est* to short adjectives. Use *more*
or *most* with longer adjectives. Never use *more* or *most*
with adjectives that end in *-er* or *-est*.

Incorrect: Baseball is the <u>most easiest</u> game to play.
Correct: Baseball is the <u>easiest</u> game to play.
Correct: Hockey is a <u>harder</u> sport than soccer.
Correct: Basketball is the <u>most challenging</u> sport I
have ever played.

Rewrite each sentence. Use adjectives correctly.
Do not add loops to **i** or **t**.

1. Ice skating is (simple) than skiing.

_____

_____

2. Sailing is (exciting) than rowing.

_____

_____

3. Football is the (popular) game at my school.

_____

_____

4. Coach said swimming is the (easy) way shape up.

_____

_____

5. Tennis is one of the (old) sports in the world.

_____

_____

© Scott Foresman - Addison Wesley

Punctuating Compound Sentences

> One way to combine two related sentences is to use a
> comma and the word *and*.

Example: Cara and I went to the video store. We rented a movie.
Cara and I went to the video store, and we rented a movie.

Combine each set of sentences by using a comma and the
word *and*. Swing the bottom loop of **g** and **y** to the left.

1. I love to read. I usually read every day after school.

_____

_____

2. Reading is my favorite hobby. Watching movies is Lucy's favorite hobby.

_____

_____

_____

3. I picture characters in my mind. I imagine settings.

_____

_____

4. Lucy loves colorful scenes. She likes funny actors.

_____

_____

5. Lucy and I read for an hour. Then we watched a movie.

_____

_____

© Scott Foresman - Addison Wesley

Listing Likenesses and Differences

When you write a comparison, you tell a reader how two or more people or things are alike. When you write a contrast, you tell a reader how two or more things are different.

Before you write a comparison or contrast, it is helpful to make a chart showing likenesses and differences. List characteristics of the two things you are comparing. Then show whether the things are alike or different for each characteristic.

	Soccer	Tennis
Popular sport	yes	yes
Team sport	yes	no
Need lessons	no	yes
Good exercise	yes	yes
Need special equipment	yes	yes
Need a special place	yes	yes

Compare or contrast two activities, such as two sports or two hobbies. Complete the chart to show likenesses and differences. Cross **T** at the top line. Cross **F** in the middle.

	Activity 1 _____	Activity 2 _____
1. _____	_____	_____
2. _____	_____	_____
3. _____	_____	_____
4. _____	_____	_____
5. _____	_____	_____

© Scott Foresman - Addison Wesley

A Comparison/Contrast Paragraph

When you write a comparison, you tell how two or more people or things are alike. When you write a contrast, you tell how two or more things are different from each other.

≡	Make a capital.
/	Make a small letter.
∧	Add something.
℘	Take out something.
⨀	Add a period.
¶	New paragraph.

Read the contrast. Mark the errors that need to be corrected. Find two comma errors and three errors in comparing with adjectives.

Sailing and rowing are both fun but they are very different. Sailing is hardest to learn. You can learn to row in five minutes. Sailing requires a sailboat and it costs a lot to buy or rent. Rowing is done in a more simpler boat with oars. All in all, sailing is a more funner sport.

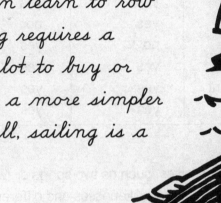

Writing Tip: Before you write, make a chart showing likenesses and differences.

Write a paragraph. Compare or contrast two activities. Be sure your writing is not too dark or too light.

© Scott Foresman - Addison Wesley

Name _____

Double Negatives

> Use only one negative word in a sentence. Remember that in contractions the *n't* stands for the word *not*.

Incorrect: You should<u>n't</u> <u>never</u> leave litter in the park.
Correct: You should <u>never</u> leave litter in the park.

Incorrect: <u>Don't</u> put <u>no</u> trash in the lake.
Correct: <u>Don't</u> put any trash in the lake.

Each sentence below has a double negative. Rewrite each sentence so it has only one negative word. Be sure to dot i's and cross t's.

1. We shouldn't never forget to recycle cans and bottles.

_____

_____

2. Many people don't never worry about wasting water.

_____

_____

3. Haven't you no ideas for saving energy?

_____

_____

4. When some resources are gone, we can't never get them back.

_____

_____

5. Some people think we can't in no way improve our environment.

_____

_____

© Scott Foresman - Addison Wesley

Name _____

Correcting Run-on Sentences

When two or more separate thoughts are written as one
sentence, a run-on results. Correct run-on sentences by
writing each complete thought as a separate sentence.
Put a period at the end of the first sentence, and start the
next sentence with a capital letter.

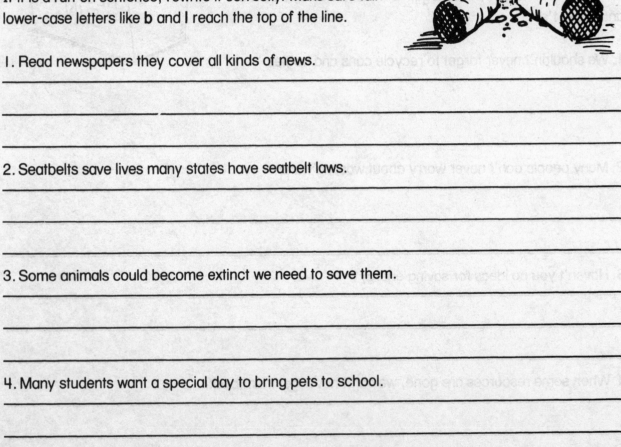

Incorrect: Our school should have a career fair
everyone wants to know more about careers.

Correct: Our school should have a career fair.
Everyone wants to know more about careers.

Read each sentence. If a sentence is correct, write *correct*.
If it is a run-on sentence, rewrite it correctly. Make sure tall
lower-case letters like **b** and **l** reach the top of the line.

1. Read newspapers they cover all kinds of news.

_____

_____

_____

2. Seatbelts save lives many states have seatbelt laws.

_____

_____

_____

3. Some animals could become extinct we need to save them.

_____

_____

_____

4. Many students want a special day to bring pets to school.

_____

_____

_____

5. Camping teaches many skills it teaches about the outdoors.

_____

_____

_____

© Scott Foresman - Addison Wesley

Name _____

Listing Facts That Support Opinions

> When you try to persuade people to support your opinion,
> you must support your opinion with good reasons.

Opinion: Recess is one of the most important times of the school day.

Supporting Reasons: 1. Students need a change from working.
2. Students need physical exercise.
3. Students need fresh air.

Write supporting reasons for each opinion.
Be sure to keep the loop open in the letter **e**.

1. All schools should teach students how to use a computer.

A. _____

B. _____

C. _____

2. Everyone should have a pet.

A. _____

B. _____

C. _____

Now write your own opinion and supporting reasons.

_____

3. Opinion: _____

A. _____

B. _____

C. _____

© Scott Foresman - Addison Wesley

A Persuasive Paragraph

When you write a persuasive paragraph, you are trying to convince your reader to agree with your opinion. You must support your opinion with good reasons. Organize your reasons in order of importance. Save your strongest reason for last.

≡	Make a capital.
/	Make a small letter.
∧	Add something.
✗	Take out something.
⊙	Add a period.
¶	New paragraph.

Read the persuasive paragraph. Mark the errors that need to be corrected. Find one double negative, two run-on sentences, and one misspelled word.

Our school district should hold a track and feild day for all four elementary schools. Our schools don't never have events together. Running races is great exercise jumping develops the leg muscles. Students could show spirit it's fun to root for your school.

Writing Tip: Support your opinion with good reasons.

Write a persuasive paragraph about something you think your school should do. Do not crowd your letters by writing them too closely together.

_____
_____
_____
_____
_____
_____
_____

© Scott Foresman - Addison Wesley

Alphabet Models

a b c d e f g h i j k l m n o
p q r s t u v w x y z
A B C D E F G H I J K L
M N O P Q R S T U V W
X Y Z

a b c d e f g h i j k l
m n o p q r s t u v w
x y z
A B C D E F G H I J K
L M N O P Q R S T U V
W X Y Z

1 2 3 4 5 6 7 8 9 10 . ? !
" " , . : ;

© Scott Foresman - Addison Wesley

Index

© Scott Foresman - Addison Wesley